PHILMONT

A Brief History of the
New Mexico Scout Ranch

PHILMONT

A Brief History of the
New Mexico Scout Ranch

by

Stephen Zimmer and Larry Walker

A Philmont Scout Ranch Book
from

Sunstone books may be purchased for educational, business, or sales promotional use. For information please write: Special Markets Department, Sunstone Press, P.O. Box 2321, Santa Fe, New Mexico 87504-2321.

FIRST EDITION

10 9 8 7 6 5 4 3 2 1

Library of Congress Cataloging-in-Publication Data:

Zimmer, Stephen.
    Philmont: a brief history of a New Mexico scout ranch / by Stephen
Zimmer and Larry Walker.
        p. cm.
    Includes bibliographical references.
    ISBN: 0-86534-293-8
        1. Philmont Scout Ranch—History. I. Walker, Larry, 1952–II. Title.
HS3313.Z65 Z55 2000
796.54'22—dc21
                                                    00-023990

Published by SUNSTONE PRESS
            Post Office Box 2321
            Santa Fe, NM 87504-2321 / USA
            (505) 988-4418 / *orders only* (800) 243-5644
            FAX (505) 988-1025
            www.sunstonepress.com

CONTENTS

Foreword / 7

Preface / 9

1 Land of the Mountain Men / 11

2 Waite Phillips and the Philmont Ranch / 24

3 Scout Camp in the Rockies / 41

4 A Ranch for Boy Scouts / 54

5 Western High Adventure / 68

6 Scouting Paradise / 111

Bibliography / 115

FOREWORD

I was four years old in 1922, when my father made the first purchase of land near Cimarron, New Mexico that later became Philmont. Our family lived in Tulsa, Oklahoma, where my father's principal business interests were, but we spent every summer and many other times at Philmont. It was a place we all enjoyed. In later years, after my sister and I had gone away to school, it was where we gathered as a family. After my sister married and had children, she often brought her two young sons to spend part of the summer on the ranch. Philmont played an important part in our family life. I literally grew up there.

From the time I went away to prep school at age fourteen until I finished college, I spent every summer vacation and most others on the ranch. I often brought school friends to visit, and they joined me in the busy routine of ranch activities.

In early summer we took our bedrolls and a string of saddle horses and joined the cow outfit. By this time my father had acquired more land, and Philmont was running more than three thousand cows. This was the time for branding calves, and for moving the cattle to summer pasture in the mountains. It was hard work. We took them in bunches of 250 to 300, trying to keep mother cows and calves together. Even then, it took some doing to get the herd "mothered up" once we reached summer pasture. There we branded the calves.

We went everywhere horseback. Each man had at least six horses in his string. It took that many to stand the 25 to 35 miles we rode each day. We changed horses sometime during each day if we could, but most of the time we were working too far from camp to get back and eat, let alone change horses.

We worked seven days a week from daylight until the work was finished. Sometimes we were through by three or four o'clock, but often it was after dark when we finally rode into camp. We seldom ate more than twice a day, but no one complained. There was something about cowboying–each man took pride in his work and his ability to withstand considerable punishment, whether riding a bucking horse or staying out all day in rain or snow. To be a part of that was a wonderful experience. I guess it spoiled me for any other line of work. I've tried other occupations, but my main interest has been ranching, and I have been at it for more than forty years.

In late summer I helped guide and entertain the friends and associates my parents invited to visit them at the ranch. My father liked to take his guests to the Rayado Lodge, where they fished and rode over the many trails he had built in the mountains. There was no road to Rayado Lodge then, so we rode in from Crater Lake, which was the end of the line for automobiles. It was a seven or eight mile ride, with all personal belongings and groceries packed on mules. It was quite a project, considering that the guests were inexperienced riders, anywhere from two years old to eighty.

Sometimes our family and a cook made up the whole party, and at other times there could be as many as twenty people along. When we got to Rayado Lodge, I helped care for the tack and horses, rigged up fishing tackle, dug worms and cleaned fish. Many of our guests were influential in business and politics. All of them were interesting, and it was a privilege for me to know them.

My father loved to ride and explore in the mountains. He always wanted to see what was on the "other side." He took an interest in trail building, and provided access to many out-of-the-way places. I was with him many times laying out a new trail, and I helped build some of them.

To say that Philmont Ranch means a lot to me is to put it mildly. It meant a lot to my father too, and I think that is one reason he gave it to the Scouts. In doing so, he acted on one of his favorite epigrams: "The only things we keep permanently are those we give away."

It makes me feel good to know of the many young people who have hiked the trails of Philmont, and of the many more who will have the same chance in years to come. I enjoy hearing about the experiences of those who have done the trail–what they have learned and what the experience has meant to them.

The authors have done a good job of putting together, in words and pictures, the story of the Philmont Ranch. This is something we have needed for a long time. The book is about a place that has meant a lot to many of us over the last sixty years or so, and it includes a variety of interesting people and events. It is true to my experience and my understanding of what has taken place before and since the time the ranch was such a big part of my growing up years. I'm glad we have this book. It is one you can read with the confidence that this is "the way it was."

—Elliott W. Phillips

PREFACE

Philmont Scout Ranch, situated in the Sangre de Cristo Mountains of northeastern New Mexico, holds an unprecedented place in Scouting circles all across America. More than 600,000 Scouts, Explorers, and their leaders have hiked its trails since its inception, and each has departed with memories of a Scouting experience that can be found no where else in the nation. The task of adequately describing Philmont in words, and what it means and has meant to those who have been there, is, to say the least, monumental. Consequently, we have opted to tell the story of Philmont primarily with pictures, thus hoping that together they will impart something of what makes the ranch such a special place to so many. If nothing else, this book constitutes the first grouping of representative historical and modern photographs of the ranch, a place that has been and will continue to be one of the most photographed areas of the American Southwest.

Compiling an historical text in association with the photographs has, of consequence, been of secondary importance in our effort. Nevertheless, it has provided an opportunity to set forth pertinent factual information surrounding the life of Philmont's benefactor, Waite Phillips, his gifts to the Boy Scouts of America, and the subsequent development and operation of the ranch as a national Scout camping area.

We are indebted to many friends for their help and encouragement in this project. Foremost among them are Mr. and Mrs. Elliott W. Phillips, son and daughter-in-law of Waite Phillips. Not only did they contribute substantial financial support to the book's previous edition, but over the years have shared with us many valuable pieces of information about Mr. Phillips and the Philmont Ranch, much of which we have incorporated in the text.

To David L. Caffey, a twelve year veteran of Philmont's summer staff, we owe a special thanks for serving as general editor of the manuscript. His thoughtful criticisms and pertinent suggestions have been of inestimable value to us. Much of what may be good about this book is due to him.

Lloyd S. Knutson, Philmont's Director of Program from 1976 to 1987, recognized early on a value in this project and is largely responsible for making its publication a reality. We learned much from him during the years we worked for him, and our lives have been made richer as a result. Most importantly, we thank him for being our friend.

To Annette Carlisle, Philmont's Librarian, we owe a debt of gratitude for which we may never be able to repay. Her perseverance in typing the many drafts of the manuscript may only be described as extraordinary. Without her enthusiasm and patience our work would have been far more difficult.

—Stephen Zimmer and Larry Walker
Cimarron, New Mexico

Land of the Mountain Men

1

"It is my belief that the romance, history, and
traditions of the country in which
the ranch is located will contribute much
toward perpetuating American idealism and
patriotism among boys from all parts of America."
—Waite Phillips, 1942

Philmont is a land rich in western romance, legend, and adventure. Many trails hiked by today's Scouts and Explorers are the same as those once used by Indians, Spaniards, mountain men, miners, lumbermen, and cowboys. The first settlers of the Philmont country were American Indians. Archaeological sites found in the North Ponil Canyon indicate that Indian people

Petroglyphs in the North Ponil Canyon.

A Jicarilla Apache man and wife.

were living in the area by the year 400 A.D. Subsisting primarily on wild food plants and game, these people later supplemented their diet by growing corn, beans, and squash in the canyon bottom. A system of flood irrigation watered the plants. These people wove intricate baskets, made cooking pots and constructed underground pit houses in which to live.

For unknown reasons, the farming people of the North Ponil abandoned the canyon by 1400 A.D. They left only the remains of their houses, broken pots, arrow points, and baskets with which to reconstruct their cultures. The rock pictures (petroglyphs) that they pecked into the canyon walls are the most visual reminder of their presence on the ranch today. After a lapse of several centuries other Indians moved into the Philmont country. Beginning in the seventeenth century the Jicarilla Apaches located campsites along the foothills and in the canyons of the ranch's east side. These Indians rode horses for hunting buffalo. From contact with the agricultural Pueblo Indians of the Rio Grande, they learned to grow corn and other crops to add to their diet. As time drew on, the Jicarillas were pushed further into Philmont's mountain canyons by Comanches and Utes, their traditional enemies from the plains.

It was in the mountains that the Spaniards, the European colonizers of New Mexico, first saw them. Spanish soldiers first crossed Philmont in 1706 in an expedition under Juan de Ulibarri, who was sent to subdue the Comanches and protect the friendly Jicarillas.

Another Spanish expedition, this time led by the governor of the province, Don Antonio de Valverde, followed Ulibarri's footsteps across Philmont in the summer of 1719. Although both expeditions failed to encounter the Comanches, they left the Jicarillas with promises to protect them in the future.

However, the Indians were left to war and raid among themselves for the next hundred years. They saw few white people until the 1820s when Americans arrived from the east and began exploring the Southwest.

The first Americans to see Philmont were trappers who came to its mountains in search of beaver. The animal's fur was used to make stylish hats worn by men in the Eastern United States and Europe.

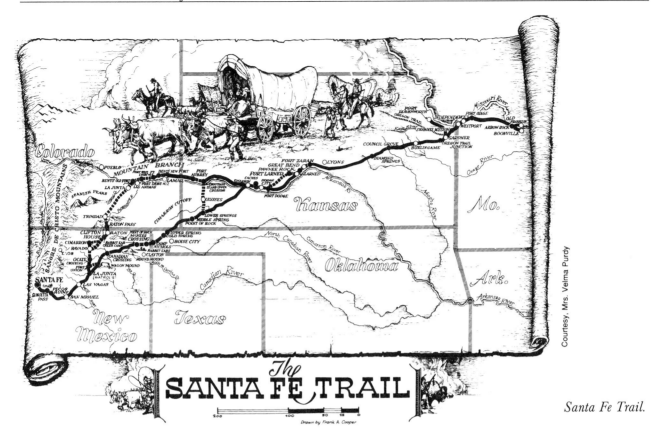

Santa Fe Trail.

Merchants arrived in the Southwest soon thereafter, bringing wagon loads of manufactured goods to trade in the New Mexican capital of Santa Fe. Starting in Missouri, they followed the Santa Fe Trail across the plains of Kansas to the Arkansas River. There the trail split, one route taking a direct southwesterly course toward Santa Fe, while the other, known as the mountain branch, continued along the Arkansas to Bent's Fort. From there it proceeded across Raton Pass and along the east side of Philmont's mountains, winding its way eventually to Santa Fe.

Among the well-known mountain men and traders who passed through Philmont on their way to Santa Fe or Taos were Kit Carson, Lucien Maxwell, William and Charles Bent, Ceran St. Vrain, Jedediah Smith, and Jim Beckwourth. At the time Philmont was still part of the Mexican province of New Mexico.

Perhaps the best known of all these men was Kit Carson, who like Daniel Boone, became a legend in his own time. Also like Boone, Carson and his exploits are surrounded by a cloud of myth and romance although the accurate details of his life provide a story of drama and heroism equal to any piece of fiction.

Kit Carson.

From Kit Carson's Life and Adventures, 1874.

In appearance Kit Carson was anything but heroic. Small and unassuming, he stood five feet, six inches tall and weighed 140 pounds. He was known for his straight forward manner and modesty in spite of his many deeds of daring and heroism. He never learned to read and write. Born in Kentucky in 1809, Carson first came to the Rocky Mountains at Taos in 1826. During a subsequent career as a beaver trapper, hunter, guide, Indian agent, and military officer he participated in many of the important events in the exploration and settlement of the American West. He came to know the mountains, plains, and deserts of the West and the Indians who inhabited them as intimately as anyone of his time. Carson died at Fort Lyon, Colorado on May 23, 1868.

In 1841, a large tract of land encompassing the present ranch was granted to two Mexican citizens, Carlos Beaubien and Guadalupe Miranda. Although they agreed to colonize the grant immediately, frontier conditions prevented settlement on it until 1848 when the area became a part of the United States as a result of the Mexican War.

In the spring of that year, Beaubien's son-in-law, Lucien Maxwell, led settlers east across the mountains from Taos to the Rayado River. The colony he started was strategically located near where a trail branched off to Taos from the Santa Fe Trail.

Although Maxwell's ranch initially suffered frequent Indian attacks, it prospered. Herds of cattle, sheep, horses, and mules were pastured and hay and other crops were raised. Kit Carson joined Maxwell as a partner in the enterprise and stayed until appointed Indian agent at Taos in 1854. A company of United States Dragoons was stationed at Rayado in 1850 and 1851. They were charged with protecting not only the fledgling colony, but traders on the Santa Fe Trail as well.

Lucien Maxwell, 1818.

Maxwell decided to establish a new ranch on the Cimarron River in 1857. Headquartered there, he expanded his operations by enlarging his cattle herds and farming extensive acreages along the river. Hundreds of men, mostly Mexicans, lived on Maxwell's Ranch, worked his fields and herded his cattle. Sometimes they were paid in money, other times they received cattle or grain for their labor. As a result, the ranch was likened by several contemporary observers to a feudal kingdom.

To grind wheat from his fields, Maxwell erected a three-story gristmill. When the United States Government established an agency for the Jicarillas and Utes on the ranch in 1861, Maxwell obtained contracts to provide them with weekly rations of flour. The mill's product was in great demand.

Jicarilla Apaches receiving rations from Maxwell's grist mill in Cimarron.

By 1864 Maxwell had acquired Miranda's share of the grant. Beaubien had died earlier that year and Maxwell began the process of buying up the claims of his heirs. Consequently, the property came to be known as the Maxwell Land Grant.

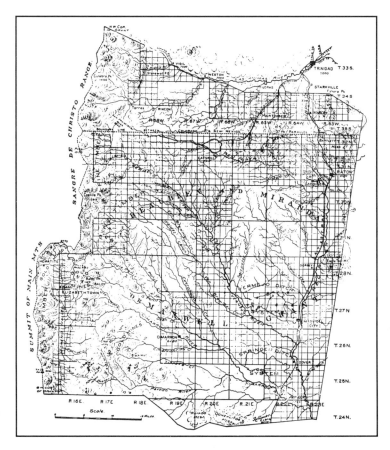

Maxwell Land Grant.

Blackhorse Mine southeast of Baldy Mountain.

Gold was discovered in the mountains of the western part of the grant in 1866. Miners rushed to the placers of the Moreno Valley and Baldy Mountain areas, and Maxwell's wealth increased as he was paid a portion of the gold mined from his land. With several partners, he opened the most productive gold mine on the grant, the Aztec, located inside the Aztec Ridge east of Baldy.

Hydraulic mining in the Moreno Valley.

Maxwell Cattle Company cowboys during roundup.

Maxwell Land Grant Company promotional brochure.

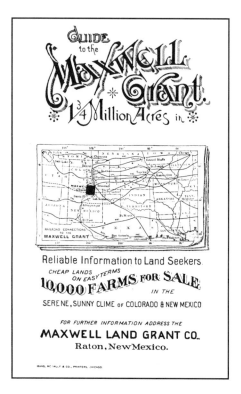

Having established a ranch kingdom of almost mythical proportions, Maxwell entered into negotiations to sell the grant in 1870. For $1,350,000 a group of English investors, who intended to sell land, mine gold, and run cattle, acquired the grant and set up the Maxwell Land Grant and Railway Company.

The company immediately encountered resistance from miners and others who had previously settled on the grant but did not hold titles to the land. Where Maxwell had allowed many to live and work on his ranch, often with no compensation, the Land Grant Company considered them squatters and insisted that they purchase their land. On the other hand, the settlers believed they were on public domain and outside the grant proper which they believed to include no more than 100,000 acres.

The ensuing fifteen years was a dark period in the history of the area. Known as the Colfax County War, the region was the scene of numerous murders for nearly two decades after Lucien Maxwell sold his land to investors. Conflict arose early between the new owners and the farmers, ranchers, and miners whom Maxwell had allowed to settle on his ranch.

Two Cimarron ministers, both of whom supported the settlers, figured prominently in the conflict; one by his death, the other by his persistence. In September of 1875, the Reverend F.J.

Ponil Canyon settlers.

Tolby, a Methodist minister and outspoken critic of the land grant company, was found murdered in Cimarron Canyon. It was assumed by many that the killer had been hired by the company. Tolby's murder set off violence that pervaded the region for the next fifteen years.

In part because of the death of his friend, another minister, the Reverend Oscar P. McMains, began a personal crusade against the land grant company. McMains' campaign lasted until the U.S. Supreme Court confirmed the right of the company to nearly two million acres in its decision of April 18, 1887. McMains made one last appeal for the settlers to President Grover Cleveland but was denied. Peace gradually came to the region after the Supreme Court's decision. Settlers either bought their land from the company or sold the improvements and left. No one is certain how many deaths were the result of the war, and most of the killings remain "unsolved" to this day.

Much of the land was already owned or was soon purchased by individuals running huge herds of cattle and sheep. Specific to what was to become Philmont were the Rayado, Urraca, Heck, and Nash Ranches. Gold mining continued under several companies primarily in the Baldy Mountain region. Maxwell's old Aztec Mine remained the most profitable, although it was operated only intermittently until World War II.

Street scene in Cimarron at the turn of the century.

Hard rock miners in the Aztec Mine during the 1920s.

Gold ore was brought from the mine by tramway.

After the turn of the 20th Century, farmers, cattlemen, and miners on the old grant came to require a way to transport their produce, cattle, and ore. Their need was met when the St. Louis, Rocky Mountain, and Pacific Railroad was built into Cimarron in 1906 continuing its way into Ute Park.

In January of 1907 Thomas A. Schomburg organized the Continental Tie and Lumber Company in Cimarron. His object was to make railroad ties and mine timbers from trees located in the Ponil canyons northwest of town. He also established the Cimarron and Northwestern Railroad as a subsidiary company to transport the timber out of the mountains.

Engine 101 of the St. Louis, Rocky Mountain, & Pacific Railway.

Loggers hauling to North Ponil sawmill.

*A Cimarron & Northwestern train
loaded with logs.*

Construction workers began laying track for the C & N through Ponil Canyon the following June. The line was built up North Ponil Canyon and was a total of twenty-two miles in length when completed. Loggers established camps and sawmills along the line and harvested the thick stands of Ponderosa pine and Douglas fir called red spruce by the lumbermen. The spruce logs were either peeled for use as mine timbers or hewn into railroad ties. The Ponderosa logs were rough cut into building lumber at the sawmills and then finished at Continental's planing mill in Cimarron.

By 1923 all of the available timber in the North Ponil Canyon had been cut. Consequently, crews took up the C & N's track and proceeded to build the line up the main Ponil Canyon into the South Ponil. Operations there centered around Pueblano until 1930 when again the timber was depleted and the track taken out.

By 1922 the stage was set for the coming of an oilman from Oklahoma. Waite Phillips was to have perhaps the greatest impact on the land known today as Philmont Scout Ranch.

Continental Tie and Lumber Company mill workers.

Baldy, New Mexico, 1920s.

2

Waite Phillips and The Philmont Ranch

"(Our) idea was to conserve the natural resources of the land both for our own use and for future posterity."
—Waite Phillips, 1948

Waite Phillips was born on a small farm near Conway, Iowa on January 19, 1883. With his identical twin brother, Wiate, he left home at age sixteen in search of adventure in the West and

Waite Phillips' family on their farm near Conway, Iowa, summer 1899.

the Rocky Mountains. For three years the Phillips twins traveled through the northern Rockies working as laborers at various mining, timber, and railroad camps. In the summer of 1902 Wiate became seriously ill from a ruptured appendix. He died in a hospital in Spokane, Washington at age nineteen.

Distraught over his brother's death, Waite returned to Iowa. With the encouragement of his older brothers, Frank and L.E., he enrolled in the business department of the Western Normal College in Shenandoah, Iowa. Upon graduation in the summer of 1903, he took a position as bookkeeper with the Hawkeye Coal Company in Knoxville where he met and married Genevieve Elliott, the daughter of a local banker. Later he was hired as a salesman for the Rex Coal and Mining Company of Creston, Iowa.

Waite and Wiate Phillips while working as Western Union messengers in Ogden, Utah, about 1920.

During this period, two of his brothers, Frank and L.E., moved to Oklahoma Territory where they invested in the developing oil business. Phillips followed them to the Oklahoma oil fields and their Bartlesville headquarters in the spring of 1906.

Phillips worked with his brothers in their oil exploration and production business until the summer of 1914. At that time, the two older brothers decided to liquidate the assets of their oil enterprises in order to devote their full energies to their banking interests.

Waite followed suit by selling his minor interest in the business and purchasing an oil marketing firm headquartered in Fayetteville, Arkansas. After operating it for a year, he sold the company and returned to the Oklahoma fields.

The Phillips family including Frank, L.E., Waite, Fred, and their mother at Frank's Woolaroc Ranch near Bartlesville, Oklahoma, mid 1930s.

A Waite Phillips Company Station in the early 1920s.

Establishing headquarters at Okmulgee, Oklahoma, Phillips developed a number of extensive oil producing properties with success and soon expanded his operation to include refining, transportation, and marketing facilities.

His brothers, in liquidating their various oil assets in 1914, were forced to retain certain oil and gas leases they held on Osage Indian land. These properties proved to be so valuable after further exploration that the brothers again entered the oil business in 1917 and established the Phillips Petroleum Company.

Waite, on the other hand, remained on his own and moved his headquarters to Tulsa in the spring of 1918. Four years later, he integrated his holdings into the Waite Phillips Company and served as its president and general manager.

In the spring of 1925, Phillips sold the capital stock of the Waite Phillips Company to Blair and Company, a Wall Street investment firm, for twenty-five million dollars cash. The sale freed him to pursue his banking and real estate investments, which included several ranches in the West.

From his youth, Phillips had always wanted to own a mountain cow ranch. As his oil investments grew and turned profits, he looked more and more into this kind of property.

In 1920, he bought a ranch near Denver that he called the Highland. Not pleased, however, with its recreational possibilities, he continued to search for a ranch with more mountainous acreage.

In the spring of 1922 Phillips learned of the proposed sale of the Urraca Ranch headquartered south of Cimarron. He dispatched his Denver ranch manager, Gene Hayward, to Cimarron to investigate and as a result of his report, Phillips purchased almost 42,000 acres of the Urraca for more than $150,000. Early in the spring of the next year, he acquired an additional 30,000 acres of the ranch for nearly one-quarter million dollars.

The Urraca Ranch, with its choice grazing and farming acres along the foothills and mountains of the Sangre de Cristo range, provided an excellent foundation property from which

The Hawkeye Ranch Gate.

Phillips was able to expand his holdings. As contiguous property became available, including mountain land owned by the Maxwell Land Grant Company, he purchased it. By 1926 he had put almost 300,000 acres under one fence.

In recognition of his native state of Iowa, Phillips initially named the ranch the Hawkeye. But in 1925, he renamed it Philmont, a derivation of his own name and the Spanish word for mountain, "monte."

George Rockenfield, Philmont Ranch farm foreman, oversees farmers mowing a field.

After acquiring the Urraca, Phillips immediately began developing the ranch's livestock, farming, and recreational resources. He brought to this work the same energy and managerial skill that had made him overwhelmingly successful in the oil business.

Of primary importance was a residence on the ranch for the Phillips family. In the summer of 1925, Phillips and his wife Genevieve, accompanied by Kansas City architect Edward B. Delk, embarked on a Mediterranean cruise with the express purpose of gathering architectural ideas for a home at Philmont and a main residence in Tulsa. Construction on both houses began in the spring of 1926. The Phillipses returned to the Mediterranean that summer and acquired the majority of furnishings that eventually went into both mansions.

The Philmont Ranch gate that stood at the present entrance to the Scout Ranch administration area.

Wiley Post (left) and Will Rodgers (right) visited Waite Phillips at the Philmont Ranch in August of 1935. Phillips is holding his grandson, Phillips Breckenridge.

A view of the Villa Philmonte before the gazebo was added in 1929.

Villa Living Room.

Dining Room.

Trophy Room.

The twenty-two room Philmont mansion was completed the following spring and was called the Villa Philmonte. It was home to the Phillips family each year from the beginning of June to the beginning of October. There they hosted friends and business acquaintances who were invited to the ranch to rest, relax, and enjoy the pleasant summer climate.

Phillips built four recreational log cabins in the mountains west of the ranch's headquarters. The largest was the Rayado Lodge located in the south part of the ranch at the confluence of the Rayado and Agua Fria Rivers. It became the most popular backcountry destination for the Phillips family and their friends. It required a two-day horseback ride which included an overnight stay at Crater Lake Lodge.

Mr. and Mrs. Phillips often invited friends and business associates to Philmont each summer to enjoy the beauty of the ranch. One noteworthy group arrived in July 1927 and was headed by United States Vice President Charles Dawes. Cartoonist John T. McCutcheon, who later drew pictures on the walls of the Villa Philmonte's Trophy Room, was a member of the party, as were novelists Ben Ames Williams and Kenneth L. Roberts. The highlight of the visit was a

Waite Phillips fishing on the Rayado River.

An interior view of the Rayado lodge (present day Fish Camp).

A view of the Rayado Lodge looking up Aqua Fria Canyon.

Visitors at Crater Lake Lodge.

Vice President Charles Dawes.

horseback and fishing trip to Rayado Lodge. Roberts recounted the group's adventures in a story titled "Hardships in New Mexico" that appeared in the December 10, 1927 issue of the *Saturday Evening Post.*

In attending to the operation of the ranch itself, Phillips was unable to draw upon a past experience in the management of cattle, sheep, or horses. He made up for his lack of experience by carefully studying all aspects of modern livestock management and adapting pertinent methods to his ranch's situation. Eventually Philmont was to run more than 3,000 head of Hereford cows and 9,000 head of Corriedale sheep.

Although an absentee owner for part of the year, Phillips kept in close touch with all activity at the ranch. He required his ranch managers to prepare and send written reports to him weekly. The reports carried information regarding weather conditions, current operations in the cow, horse, sheep, and farm departments, plus pertinent items dealing with personnel, water, and fences. Phillips was meticulous in responding to each of the reports and offered suggestions for particular action and possible solutions to problems.

Philmont Ranch advertisement in the Denver Record Stockman, 1937.

Philmont Ranch employee, Hipilito Casias.

No aspect of the ranch's operation escaped the owner's attention. Phillips was especially concerned with the welfare of his employees. On the average, the ranch employed as many as fifty people; including ten cowboys, fifteen sheepherders, twenty farmers, plus maintenance and office personnel. Each employee

Melaquias Epinosa, Philmont Ranch cowboy.

with a family was supplied a house, milk cow, garden seed, poultry stock, beef and pork. In a letter to his ranch manager in May of 1936, Phillips stated that the ranch furnished "to its employees as nearly as possible, what they would receive if they owned or leased a small place of their own."

Perhaps the greatest contribution Phillips made to the success of the ranch's operation was his plan for the management of the cow herd and its efficient utilization of the available range grass. This plan involved developing springs and using cross fences and strategic salt distributions in pastures in order to entice cattle to graze inaccessible parts of the ranch.

In addition, Phillips instructed the cow and sheep employees to kill grass-eating gophers wherever they were found. He had them dig loco weed in the foothills and mountain parks each spring as it began to grow and threaten livestock.

Beaver found on the ranch were used to help improve range conditions. Phillips had employees live-trap beaver that resided along streams running through winter calving pastures where the animals destroyed much of the cover important in

Branding Philmont calves at Aqua Fria Park, summer, 1927. The boy in the foreground is Elliot Phillips.

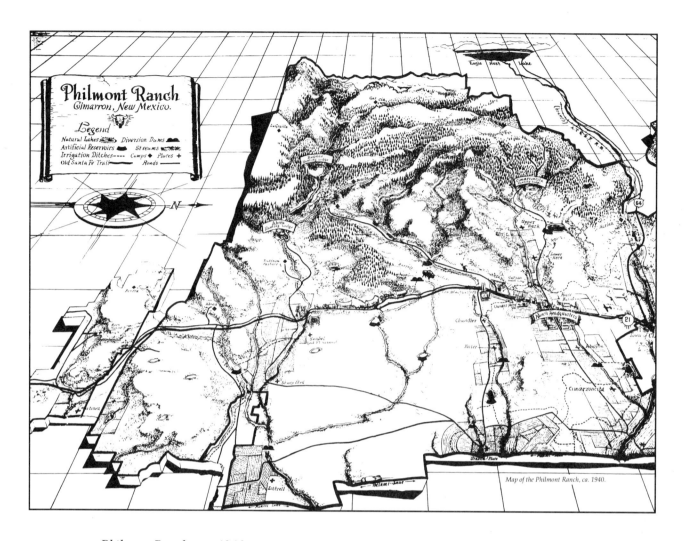

Philmont Ranch, ca. 1940.

*Loading Philmont Ranch calves onto
Santa Fe Railroad cars in Cimarron.*

sheltering cows during calving season. After capture, the beaver were transported to mountain parks where they cut down aspen and thus created better growing conditions for grass. Also, their dams promoted the formation of siltation areas that eventually grassed over.

Philmont cows, bearing the ranch's UU Bar brand, bore their calves each spring, generally from the middle of March to the middle of May, while pastured on the sheltered lowlands. Sometime during the first part of June, the cowboys began gathering cows and calves and pushing them to Zastro cow camp. From Zastro they were started in bunches of roughly 300 head along with the herd bulls up the cow drive to the summer mountain pastures of La Grulla, Agua Fria, and Garcia Parks. The older cows seldom needed encouragement to climb on top, having been conditioned by making many previous drives.

Garcia Cow Camp on the Philmont Ranch, located on the present day UU Bar Ranch.

Waite Phillips and cowboys at the Rayado Lodge.

Waite Phillips and one of his favorite trail horses, Zack.

At the top of the drive, the cows were met by another crew of cowboys who held them at La Grulla Park and branded the calves. Following branding, the cattle were pushed to the western extent of the pastures and then allowed to drift back eastward to the lower elevations of the parks as the summer progressed.

View of Tooth Ridge from the Villa Gazebo.

All the cows, calves, and bulls were gathered from the high country by the end of September. After the calves were weaned in October, they were driven to Cimarron, loaded on a branch line of the Santa Fe railroad, and shipped to market in Kansas City.

Philmont's horse breeding program was renowned for the variety, quality, and versatility of the foals it produced. Thoroughbred, Steeldust (Quarter Horse), and Percheron sires all stood at the ranch. Depending on what broodmares they were crossed on, these stallions sired colts capable of working cows, playing polo, serving as cavalry mounts, or pulling wagons and farm equipment.

The most famous Philmont horse was a Palomino sire named Plaudit. His sons and daughters consistently showed his excellent disposition, conformation, speed and often his color and were popular with breeders all over the West. Two of his most famous sons were the Quarter Horse greats, Question Mark and Scooter W.

Waite Phillips in the Villa auto court.

By 1938 the Philmont Ranch was recognized as one of the best ranch properties in the American West. Phillips made plans that year to share part of the vast ranch with others.

Scout Camp in the Rockies

"To give money and property away without plans, thought, and effort is easy but to do it right is a hard job."
—Waite Phillips, 1943

Waite Phillips once wrote that "real philanthropy consists of helping others, outside our own family circle, from whom no thanks is expected or required." He demonstrated this belief by making substantial financial contributions to various Tulsa charitable organizations and by providing capital funds for building projects undertaken by other educational, religious, and welfare institutions.

Waite Phillips in his Philtower office.

The Villa Philbrook, Tulsa, Oklahoma.

In October of 1938, he and Mrs. Phillips directed the founding of the Southwest Art Association as a corporate organization to receive the gift of their palatial estate, the Villa Philbrook. Their interest in art and culture led to this donation with the intent that the home be transformed into an art museum for the people of Tulsa and the Southwest.

Earlier that year Phillips had written the President of the Boy Scouts of America, Walter W. Head, with a proposal to donate a portion of the Philmont Ranch to the organization. He felt that a successful wilderness camp might be established by the BSA on a part of the ranch. In his letter he invited Head and other officials to come to Cimarron to inspect the property he had in mind.

An advance party, including L.L. McDonald, National Director of Camping, Ray H. Bryan, Assistant Director of Engineering Service, and Regional Scout Executive James P. Fitch, was dispatched to Philmont by Dr. James E. West, the Chief Scout Executive. The men spent two days horseback, primarily in the Ponil country, the area Phillips felt most suitable for a Scout camping operation. They were later joined by West, Head, and Arthur A. Shuck, Director of the BSA's Division of Operations.

The group discussed at length various ways the property might be developed and used. Phillips was particularly pleased with the enthusiasm expressed by the group over the proposed site and its potential as a camping area. He especially liked Fitch's assessment that the property represented an opportunity for the BSA to establish a great university of the outdoors unlike anything else in the movement. As he indicated later, Phillips' final decision to make the donation was largely a result of the party's favorable response. He was pleased with the appraisal of the property's potential value to older members of the Scouting organization.

On October 7th, Phillips wrote President Head to confirm his previous oral commitment to donate 35,857 acres of the Ponil country together with $50,000 to be used in establishing a camp headquarters. His only stipulation was that the land be used for the benefit of members of the Boy Scouts of America.

The entrance to Philturn at Six-Mile Gate, Ponil Canyon.

Phillips suggested that he thought a logical site for a headquarters was Five Points, a spot where the South, Middle, and Main Ponil Canyons converged with Horse and Trail Canyons. He felt that trails extending from that point with additional ones leading to Bear Canyon and the North Ponil would provide full access to the property. He suggested that the camp be designated a game preserve to allow campers the opportunity to observe the abundant deer, turkey, bear, and other wildlife of the area.

Some discussion had already transpired regarding a suitable name for the camp. Phillips stated that, although a specific name was not involved in any part of the proposal, he was agreeable to combining part of his name, "Phil," with "turn" indicative of the Scout slogan, "Do a good turn daily." He thereby proposed Philturn Boy Scout Park or a similar combination that would serve the organization's needs.

Finally he stated, "If this proposal were being made to any other organization, whose rating was inferior to that record of service made by the Boy Scouts of America, I would be inclined

Philturn map from the 1941 promotional brochure.

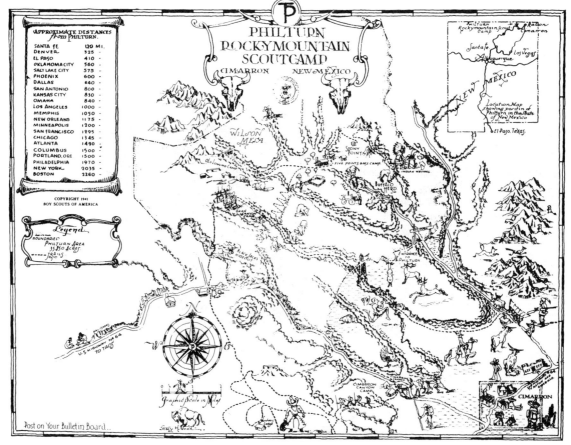

to be more particular in outlining a program, to be assured that the property would be put to full beneficial use as I visualize it, but I feel amply assured as a result of your record and in my contacts and conversations with you all, that the Executives and the Advisory Board will not accept this property and cash gift unless they feel that it will be beneficial to the Scout program and that the National Council will provide ways and means for financing its complete development and its operations in the interest of enduring betterment to the youth of America."

Dr. West thereafter issued a statement to the National Executive Board describing the history and physical features of the proposed gift. In part it read, "Each of the canyons is of the same general makeup, flanked on each side by ever changing vistas, rock palisades, timber growth, and with smaller canyons in endless numbers fingering out from the main ones. There are also several high land meadows or mesas, offering excellent additional camping spots. Bear Canyon, Dean Canyon, and Turkey Canyon have an extensive amount of timber growth, comprised principally of western pines, Douglas fir, balsam, quaking aspens and cottonwoods. It is the natural habitat of deer and while on the property we saw mule deer, wild turkeys, and dozens of beaver dams and many evidences of bear."

The Philturn commissary.

He further stated that "while there are few Boy Scout Local Councils throughout the country which do not have camps both for short camping trips and for summer vacation camping, there is a need of opportunities for Troops and Patrols with experience, training, leadership and proper equipment to secure the benefits of wilderness camping, which I believe will appeal to older boys in all parts of America. By this is implied a more rugged experience with 'nature in the raw' than is possible in the customary local Boy Scout Council camp but at no sacrifice of our essential safeguards of health and safety."

His words were to signal the philosophy under which the Phillips ranch properties have operated since.

The National Executive Board officially accepted the gift on October 20th and in December adopted Philturn Rockymountain Scoutcamp as its name. B.B. Dawson, Scout Executive at Lincoln, Nebraska was appointed director. His twenty-one years as Scout Executive with councils in Missouri, Kansas, and Nebraska, coupled with his broad experience directing various Scout camps made him a logical choice to develop the new camp.

Philturn Scouts cooking.

Plans were immediately set in motion to open Philturn in the summer of 1939. Before June, three troop camping sites were constructed at Five Points along with a Director's cabin and a commissary building. Cooking shelters and fireplaces were built in Dean Canyon, at Pueblano, and on Stony Point. Burros and saddle horses were purchased and readied for the upcoming camping season.

Equally important, specific camping policies were established. Because Philturn was considered from the beginning as a laboratory for adventure camping for Senior Scouts, the minimum age requirement was set at fifteen years old. Further, campers were required to demonstrate, to the satisfaction of local council officials, camping ability and experience adequate to Philturn's wilderness conditions.

From the beginning Philturn officials felt that Scouts would derive the greatest benefit from camping on the property if they were encouraged to design their own activities while at the ranch. The headquarters, therefore, was to be a staging and outfitting area from which each group would embark to outlying parts of the camp. Each group would provide its own leadership. A group could choose to spend its entire stay backpacking; but it was also possible to incorporate horse rides or burro packing as part of the experience. A group could also choose to take along one of the camp's chuckwagons and a cook.

Gold panning on the Ponil.

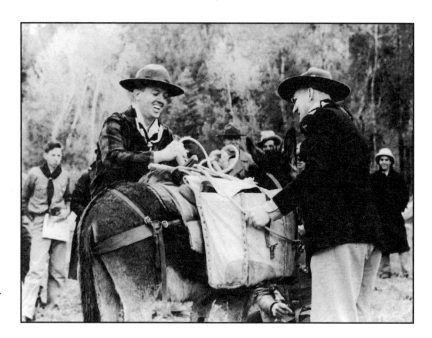

A burro packing demonstration.

Scouts at lunch at a Philturn chuckwagon.

A variety of organized exploration trips were also offered. Scouts could choose either a three day backpack trip, an expedition, or an overnight horseback ride. Some groups chose to participate in longer excursions of six or twelve days. These involved activities at Philturn, and side trips to nearby historic and scenic sites like Mount Capulin, the Carson National Forest, Cimarron Canyon, and Taos Pueblo.

The weekly rate per camper was set at $1.00, with additional fees for meals, horses, and guide service related to longer explorations. Each group was expected to provide its own tenting and cooking equipment, although tents, blankets, and cowboy sleeping tarps were available at the camp.

A concerted effort was made to publicize the opportunities at Philturn to Scout Executives across the nation and to their boys and leaders. Articles appearing in Scouting and Boy's Life detailed the camp's facilities and programs and emphasized its wilderness backcountry where so many historic characters had once roamed.

Leaving Philturn horseback.

The main lodge at Philturn.

A rest stop on Stony Point.

In spite of such promotion, only 189 Scouts from Texas, Kansas, Louisiana, and Oklahoma were able to make arrangements to camp at Philturn the first summer. Nevertheless, construction began in the fall on a headquarters complex at Five Points, including a main lodge to house a kitchen, dining room, and director's office. By the beginning of the 1940 season, three

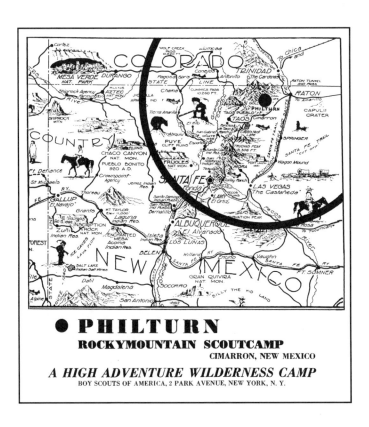

*The cover of the 1940 Philturn
promotional brochure.*

stone camping shelters had also been erected. Dawson wrote, "For every Scout or leader who attended during the 1939 season, more than four attended during the season of 1940." National Council Executives were pleased with the response noting the increase in the number of councils that had sent Scouts to Philturn. As was hoped, the camp's program was stimulating troops to try adventure camping, while helping hold the interest of older boys in Scouting.

The 1941 season opened with the addition of a director's residence and guest house. Also, a building called the "longhouse" had been constructed at the mouth of Horse Canyon. It was designated for use by staff during the summer, but more importantly it was to serve as a headquarters for Scoutmasters participating in training courses during the spring and fall. The curriculum developed for these courses was to be designed to not only familiarize leaders with the camp and its program, but to inspire them to bring expeditions of their own in the future. The cost of these buildings and other improvements came to $22,000 of which Waite Phillips agreed to pay half.

One group that camped at Philturn in the summer of 1941 called themselves the Philturn Archaeological Expedition. Under the leadership of Samuel D. Bogan, Scout Executive of Quinnipiac Council, the six Connecticut Scouts had studied archaeological methods for several months before arriving. They came specifically to investigate prehistoric Indian sites in the North Ponil Canyon.

Excavating Box Canyon Rock Shelter.

Philturn Scouts and teepees.

The boys explored the canyon for fourteen days and located many sites. They dug several of them with trowels and shovels. Each one was meticulously mapped and the excavated artifacts were systematically cataloged. Bogan kept a journal of their camp and published an account of the group's adventure in 1946 that he titled, *Let the Coyotes Howl.* In it he not only recorded the results of the archaeological work but devoted many pages to his Scouts and what they learned and how they grew while camping in the mountains. His reflections are not unlike what other leaders have discovered about their own Scouts in countless Philmont expeditions since.

Waite Phillip's favorite horse, Gus.

Phillips was interested in more than facilities at Philturn. He frequently met with Dawson and discussed the camp's operation, sometimes taking the director on horseback rides to point out a particular trail or scenic area that he felt might be included in the program.

He often drove to Philturn and sat quietly in his car observing the Scouts in camp. Other times he rode his favorite horse, Gus, among the boys as they made their camps and hiked the trails. Phillips rarely made his identity known, but took the opportunity to learn first hand how they were enjoying themselves. He believed these visits to be the best way to determine the impact of Philturn on the people it was intended to benefit.

Phillips evidently liked what he saw, for he soon contacted Scout officials about an additional donation, a gift much larger than the first and destined to be of far greater consequence in its benefit to the members of the Scouting movement.

4 A Ranch for Boy Scouts

**"...the benefits to be derived from such
a program look so big and useful that it
transcends any element of personality
or any individual who may have anything
to do with bringing it into being."**
—Waite Phillips, 1941

In the fall of 1941, Waite Phillips met with Walter Head, James West, and Arthur Shuck in St. Louis where Phillips presented a tentative proposal for donating a much larger part of the Philmont Ranch to the Boy Scouts of America. In a later meeting at the ranch, he outlined in detail the particulars of the gift he was considering. It included 91,538 acres of mountainous

Scouts horseback on the Tooth of Time Ridge.

backcountry plus the Villa Philmonte and the buildings and facilities at the ranch headquarters. Because he felt that American Scouts and their leaders would benefit from educational opportunities deriving from a diversified western ranch, he offered to include herds of beef and dairy cattle, sheep, horses, and buffalo, plus hog and poultry stock as part of the gift.

Phillips knew that substantial funds would be necessary for developing and operating a camping operation on the enlarged area. He therefore offered the 23-story Philtower Building in Tulsa as part of his proposal. The building was then netting $130,000 annually in office rentals, and the properties were valued at more than five million dollars.

The BSA men were astonished at the immensity and generosity of Phillips' offer. They immediately recognized many possibilities for an expanded camping program on the property, given the many miles of trail and the four mountain lodges Phillips had already built there.

However, they were concerned with how such valuable properties might best be managed for the benefit of the members of the organization and to meet the intent in which they were given. Phillips assured them he would be available in the upcoming months to assist in developing a management plan. Consequently, they made ready to have the proposal brought before the BSA National Executive Board at their December 18th meeting in New York.

The Philtower Building, Tulsa, Oklahoma.

Elliot Phillips riding in Rayado Canyon, summer 1933.

Armed with Phillips' letter of December 11 describing the proposed gifts, President Head presented the specifics to the Board and gained their unanimous acceptance. It was agreed to consolidate the new ranch property with Philturn and call the whole, Philmont Scout Ranch, when it was officially transferred on December 31st. The result of the Board's action was announced to the press on December 19th by Phillips in Tulsa and Head in New York.

In his statement to the *Tulsa Daily World,* Phillips was quoted as saying, "That ranch represents an ideal of my youth . . . and has meant a lot to my son and his pals. Now I want to make it available to other boys . . . I'd be selfish to hold it for my individual use."

As with Philturn, Phillips imposed no restrictions on the BSA regarding the gifts beyond that they be used "for the advancement and development of the program of Scouting." He did, however, state that although he did not "want to make any demand upon the Boy Scouts of America . . . for twenty

The entrance to Philmont's Camping Headquarters in 1944.

consecutive years, (the) ranch has been a part of my life. My son grew to manhood there. I would like to reserve for myself and members of my family the right to walk or ride over this property." He further requested that his horse, Gus, be turned out on the ranch, unridden, to live out his life in fields "white with clover."

Drawing from experience in managing the two properties, Phillips suggested that the BSA appoint a general manager with overall responsibility for operations at both the ranch and Philtower. He further advised that operations be departmentalized into ranching and recreation divisions with superintendents over each. Likewise, he recommended that the Philtower retain its own superintendent who would also report to the general manager.

BSA officials acted upon his suggestions by naming Clyde King of Tulsa as general manager of both

Scouts gathered around a New Mexico state historical marker, early 1940s.

properties. B.B. Dawson continued as Director of Camping over the enlarged acreage and Roy A. Cartwright, the current Philmont Ranch manager, agreed to assume the same responsibility for the Scouts. Louis H. Moses also agreed to remain in his position as manager of the Philtower Building.

The official announcement of the gifts to the Scouting movement was published in the January, 1942 issue of Scouting, which quoted Waite Phillips' reasons for giving them to the BSA.

"In viewing conditions today, I am impressed with the responsibility of this generation to adequately train its youth—physically, mentally, and morally—to meet the problems they must face in the future. It is my opinion that nothing can be more valuable to this generation than to enlarge this Scouting program, which develops initiative, self reliance, and dependability."

"It has always been my belief that the best contribution to that kind of development is by living close to nature and through learning to live in the great out-of-doors. It is also my belief that the romance, history, and traditions of the country in which the ranch is located will contribute much toward perpetuating American idealism and patriotism among boys from all parts of America and it is with these thoughts that I felt impelled to furnish an endowment so that all Boy Scouts and their leaders—now totaling approximately 1,500,000—would have an equal opportunity to participate."

"To summarize is to say—the proper training of the American boy is today the most urgent duty of the American adult—the Boy Scouts of America has the most efficient plan and organization to do such work—the environment of a well developed Mountain Ranch is the best place to achieve this objective."

Work began early in the spring of 1942 to prepare the Philmont Ranch for its first season as a Scout camp. It was decided to adapt the buildings of Phillips' ranch headquarters as the center of operations. The Carson Place, situated one-half mile south of the Villa, was chosen as the site of Camping Headquarters.

An early mode of transportation to Philmont.

At the Carson Place one stable was rebuilt as a dining hall, while another was converted into staff quarters. Another building was adapted as a health lodge and new stables were built on the west side of the complex.

Scouts by the Villa pool.

In the backcountry troop camping sites, stables, and corrals were built at Phillips' Abreu and Cimarroncito lodges. There, and at Ponil, Scout troops were invited to camp for extended

Campers eating at Lookout Mountain Base camp (Rayado Lodge), about 1946.

Scouts building a backcountry cabin in the early 1940s.

periods with their younger members. Along with general camping and hiking, these campers could also ride horses and pack burros. The fee was $1.00 per camper per week.

The camping program instituted for older Scouts followed to a large extent that previously offered at Philturn. Groups were encouraged to develop their own hiking and exploring activity for one or two week periods using the more than 200 miles of existing trail.

Other Senior Scouts participated in scheduled six and twelve day trips similar to those offered earlier at Philturn. These trips included backpacking, burro packing, and horseback riding accompanied by a chuckwagon and cook. The fees for each camper covered a guide and equipment, and were $9.00 for the six day trek and $18.00 for the longer stay.

In spite of all preparation, only 275 Scouts camped at Philmont its first season. America's involvement in World War II had caused many Scout leaders to join the effort and prevented them from bringing boys to the ranch.

Important administrative changes occurred the next spring when Clyde King resigned as general manager of the Philmont properties in March. Minor Huffman, a Region 9 Deputy Regional Scout Executive, was chosen to be the resident manager with responsibilities for both ranching and camping operations.

Ready for the trail at Camping Headquarters, 1944.

The fight in Europe and the Pacific produced even greater consequences for Philmont during the 1943 season. Due to conditions created by the war, the National Council decided to limit camping opportunities at Philmont for 1943 and until the national situation changed. The program brochures for that year stated that invitations to camp at the ranch would not be extended to American Scouts generally because railroad and bus lines in the West were needed for the more important movement of men and freight involved with the war. Moreover, as the National Council had committed its total support to the war effort, Scouts and their leaders were asked to stay home and participate in local projects related to it.

The Scouts that did come to Philmont came from nearby councils and were recruited as a Service Corps to build new trails and campsites and to do ranch and conservation work. Other local boys participated in a four week Senior Scout Training Camp that concentrated on teaching leadership, camping, and pioneering skills on a troop and patrol basis.

The 1943 brochure ended on a positive note, however, by encouraging Scouts and their leaders to develop long range plans to come to Philmont when travel restrictions were discontinued and facilities and trails were more fully developed.

Even with travel restrictions, participation in troop camping by Scouts from nearby councils and in Senior Scout Training

Cover of Philmont's 1943 brochure.

Minor Huffman, Philmont's manager from 1942 to 1946, with his favorite horse, Frisco.

increased each remaining year of the war. Food stuffs were often difficult to obtain from the outside, but with the help of members of the Service Corps, the ranch was able to supply most of its needs. Scouts worked in the orchard, garden and dairy and assisted in the hayfields and with the cattle acquiring the practical ranch experience Waite Phillips had envisioned.

It was at this time that Chief Scout Executive Dr. E.K. Fretwell chose a red wool shirt as the official Philmont shirt in 1944. Later he designed a black bull emblem for the shirt patterned after the bull (steer) found in the tile mosaic located at the downstairs entrance to the Villa Philmonte. In the beginning a first year camper or leader received only the head of the bull to sew over the left pocket of the shirt. After another year's participation one qualified for the body portion of the bull, and with three years, the tail. Later, the bull was made in one piece, black for men and white for women, and the shirt was changed

Members of the Philmont Service Corps in the ranch hayfields.

Service Corps Scouts pick apples in George Websters's old orchard.

to a red wool jacket. Both have become important symbols of participation at Philmont.

In keeping with Philmont's rugged terrain and advanced camping program, a minimum age of fifteen was again established for participating Scouts in 1945. An exception was made for local Scout troops that were invited to the ranch because they had no council camps of their own.

In the Ranch Garden.

*Philmont cowboy, Shorty Martinez,
discusses the fine points of the
ranch's Hereford bulls with a
Service Corps Scout.*

To replace Clyde King, the BSA selected James Fitch as manager of Phillips Properties in March of 1946. He had served as the Regional Scout Executive of Region 9 for more than twenty years and had been instrumental in negotiating with Waite Phillips regarding the gifts and in developing the camping program at both Philturn and Philmont.

With the war over, Scouts came from all twelve Regions during the 1946 season. The brochure for that year ran the slogan, "Scouting—Our only program" and offered two primary experiences. The Senior Training Program continued, accepting 429 campers compared to 76 in 1942. Its increasing popularity stemmed from the advanced curriculum of outdoor skills training. The experience prepared Scouts to assist their leaders in developing a more extensive camping program in their home units.

Working out of campsites at Rayado Rancho Base Camp, members of each Senior Training group spent the first week learning axemanship, cooking, packing, horsemanship, pioneering, stalking, nature study, and marksmanship. The second week was spent at Ponil Base Camp where, after learning how to pack burros, they took them on exploring expeditions of the surrounding canyons.

Philmont Horse foreman, Tommy Crenshaw, brands a horse.

The following week found the Scouts at Lookout Mountain Base Camp (Phillips' Rayado Lodge), where the highlight was a hike to the top of Clear Creek Mountain, the highest peak on the ranch. Finally, the Seniors were assigned horses and saddles for a week of riding at Black Mountain Base Camp (Cimarroncito).

The Exploration Program consisted of one week of hiking and burro packing, Indian lore, nature study at Ponil and another week at Abreu Base Camp riding horses and fishing. The program ended with a three day backpacking trip to Clear Creek Mountain.

During this time period, a seventeen-year-old Scout, John Westfall was camped one night in 1945 at Cimarroncito with fellow Explorers from Independence, Kansas. Inspired by the setting, he penned a poem he called, "Silver on the Sage." Later, he put music to the words during the train trip back to his home. He returned to Philmont in 1947 as a Ranger at Visto Grande camp. There he taught the words of his song to campers each evening as they sat around the campfire. The song was soon shared with everyone who came to the ranch. As it embodied so well everyone's feelings about Philmont, it was eventually adopted as "The Philmont Hymn."

Packing a burro under the watchful eye of a Philmont Cowboy.

Years later Westfall wrote about the song he created, "It's a great thrill to me to have left a little of myself in the happy memories of thousands of young people over these years as they think of their Philmont experience. Philmont is truly "God's Country" and perhaps those words and the tune I wrote will carry them back to those happy times and mountain places as it does me."

Minor Huffman resigned as Philmont's Manager in December 1946 to become the Scout Executive of the Sam Houston Area Council. Under his able leadership, the ranch had come through the difficult war years with an expanded program, well designed camping facilities, and increased participation. Huffman was succeeded by George Bullock, who was to build upon the foundation laid by his predecessor and bring Philmont to the forefront of Scouting's outdoor program.

Popular Philmont staff members from the 1940s, Tiny Williams and Frank Hopkins.

5

Western High Adventure

**"Put a boy in touch with nature
and the job of inspiring him with high ideals
is an easier one than in any other environment."
—Waite Phillips**

As Philmont's Director of Camping and Training, George Bullock introduced an even wider range of backcountry camping experiences. Recognizing the strong appeal that the history of the Cimarron country had for Scouts and their leaders,

The corrals and cabin at Beaubien.

he projected each program as a "he-man" Western adventure in the "land of the mountain men." He referred to the programs as "schedules" and gave them names like Wagon Train, Cavalcade, and Kit Carson trek, filling them with horseback riding, burro packing, dutch oven cooking, and training in mountain camping, pioneering, and hiking.

The Wagon Train was the longest schedule, consisting of twenty-three days on the trail. It was essentially the same as the previous Senior Training program and was made up of three outfits of eleven members each. The schedule started at Rayado which had been renamed Carson-Maxwell Base Camp. The first five days were spent on horsemanship, packing, cooking, hiking, and trail first aid instruction. Next followed a horseback ride with a chuckwagon to Abreu and then a hike up the canyon to Rayado Lodge for a camp of five days that culminated in a backpack trip to Clear Creek Mountain.

From Rayado, Wagon Train outfits packed their gear on burros and headed north, eventually camping at Cimarroncito.

George Bullock, Philmont's Camping Director from 1947 to 1954.

After hikes to Cypher's Mine, Deer Lake Mesa, and Hidden Valley, they again took burros and headed northward to the Bench. The schedule ended at Bent Base Camp on the Ponil with horseback rides over the surrounding canyon country and a hike to the petroglyphs in the North Ponil. The final night was spent at a buffalo banquet and awards ceremony at headquarters.

Philmont Expeditions lasted thirteen days but still covered almost 80 miles of the backcountry. They were designated as South-bound or Northbound and started at Ponil or Camping Headquarters. Following a day of visiting the Villa Philmonte and Carson-Maxwell to learn about Philmont's history, expedition campers hit the trail with gear packed on burros. A Philmont Guide was assigned to each Expedition to teach nature lore and the "Philmont Way" of camping and hiking. A highlight of the program was a layover at Cimarroncito, the crossroads of the ranch. There expedition members swapped stories and patches with campers from other schedules.

In 1949, the Boy Scouts of America instituted the Exploring Program for boys fourteen years of age or older. The Kit Carson Trek was established the same year as a special activity for Explorer posts or Senior Units of Explorers attached to Scout troops. The schedule was unusual for that time. It was done entirely with backpacks and included no burro packing or horseback riding. It had the further distinction of featuring climbs on Philmont's five highest peaks as part of the itinerary. Each trek started at the Stockade, a replica frontier log fort built near the Tooth of Time.

"Philmont or Bust," North Carolina Campers arrive at Camping Headquarters.

On the other hand, the Philmont Cavalcade offered campers a backcountry trip carried out entirely on horseback with all gear packed on horses. Included in the six day ride were side hikes to Cypher's Mine and Hidden Valley, fishing on the Rayado River, and nature study at Carson-Maxwell.

All schedules were primarily made up of either chartered or provisional council units, although individual Explorers could join any trek. For the especially ambitious camper, the

Michigan Explorers study maps of the backcountry before hitting the trail.

Frontiersman program offered participation in all four major schedules and took eight weeks to complete.

Training and work programs remained an important part of the Philmont program. The Junior Leader Training Troop was designed to prepare participants to take leadership roles in teaching Scoutcraft and the patrol method in their home units.

The 1951 Program brochure.

A Northbound Expedition on the trail.

The thirty-six day course was divided into four parts, starting with formal study in leadership methods, troop and post organization, and camping skills. After trainees were taught the techniques of teaching those skills, they put their knowledge to test by living the patrol method for one week in camp. Finally, they designed nature lore, Scoutcraft skills, and service projects for use in their home units.

The Ranch Pioneering Trek was an expanded version of the previous Service Corps program. For thirty days Explorers worked in the ranch department and built trails, cabins, and worked on conservation projects. The last week was spent on a hike through the backcountry with a Philmont Guide and pack burros.

Bullock also instituted a personal recognition program for participants, based on demonstrated competence in certain outdoor skills. A camper could qualify as a Philmont Horseman, Conservationist, Naturalist, Woodsman, Camper, or Sportsman after completing specified requirements to the satisfaction of his advisor. The requirements were so extensive that only participants in the longer Wagon Train or Junior Leader Training Camp had time to complete them all. Generally, a camper had to participate in several schedules before he could

Chief Scout Executive E. K. Fretwell, Waite Phillips, and Arthur Schuck at Philmont.

finish the requirements for each. On successful completion of each skill, the Scout was awarded an embroidered segment emblematic of his accomplishment. Each strip was sewn to the outside of the circular Philmont Award.

Lawrence "Boss" Sanchez (on the right), a Philmont cowboy for more than forty years, demonstrates throwing a diamond hitch in the early 1950s.

The Tooth of Time from Crater Lake.

In addition, Philmont campers who participated in three different schedules or who came to the ranch three different seasons could qualify for the Mountain Man award, a special recognition based on tenure. The "We All Made It" plaque was

The Stockade, where Kit Carson Treks outfitted for the trail.

first awarded in 1952. It recognized each Philmont outfit whose entire membership successfully completed the schedule. It remains an important crew recognition today.

When Waite Phillips gave Philmont to the Boy Scouts he urged Scout officials to reconstruct Kit Carson's adobe home at Rayado. A floor plan was drawn using information supplied by descendants of Lucien Maxwell's family. During the late 1940s Scouts who camped at Rayado helped make adobe bricks for the reconstruction. Workers from Taos began rebuilding the home in 1949 and completed it the following spring. It was dedicated in the summer of 1950. In detail, it was authentic to haciendas (homes) built in New Mexico in the 1850s. It included a fortified bell tower (torreon), a blacksmith shop, and a ceiling supported by pine log vigas (beams).

From the beginning it was used as a museum where campers could learn about Kit Carson's and Lucien Maxwell's contribution to the settlement of the Beaubien and Miranda Land Grant as well as get a glimpse of what life would have been like during their time at Rayado.

As Philmont's camping and hiking programs grew more popular with Scouts and Explorers, attendance increased dramatically. By 1950 campers were coming to the ranch from almost every council in the United States. Attendance had increased to over 1,700 , but by 1951 it had jumped to more than 5,200.

Hiking back to Headquarters.

*The ruins of Kit Carson's adobe at
Rayado in the 1940s.*

*Carson's home
after
reconstruction.*

A cavalcade at Lover's Leap.

Waite Phillips during a visit to Beaubien's Trappers Lodge in 1950.

A typical PTC family relaxing in their tent, 1950s.

Scouters in conference.

In keeping with Waite Phillips' wishes, adult training at Philmont was a high priority from the very beginning. Training courses were only randomly offered to Scouters at the ranch until 1950 when an official Training Center was established and headquartered at the Villa. The goal was to train a select number of Scouters from across the nation who could train other leaders in their councils back home.

On the archery line.

Family horseback ride.

In 1951 the course offering was expanded to include pack, troop, and Explorer leader training as well as several professional conferences. An experimental tent city was erected so that volunteers could bring their families with them and thereby incorporate a week of vacation with their Scout training.

The Tooth of Time belt buckle was designed in the late 1940s.

In 1957 Philmont's Director of Camping, Jack Rhea, and campcraft instructor, Doc Loomis, collaborated on a plan for sending staff members called Rangers along with campers for the first few days of their treks. The Rangers were responsible for getting crews outfitted and teaching them camping and hiking skills. They also discussed various historical events that had occurred on the ranch and pointed out flowers, plants, and geologic features while on the trail.

Waite Phillips with Ray Bryan on the Villa lawn during his last visit to the ranch in 1955.

Baldy Mountain

Fish Camp

Beaubien Camp

Scouts in meadow

gold panning

tents at Baldy

mountain panorama

Baldy and snow

Mount Phillips

cowboy

buffalo

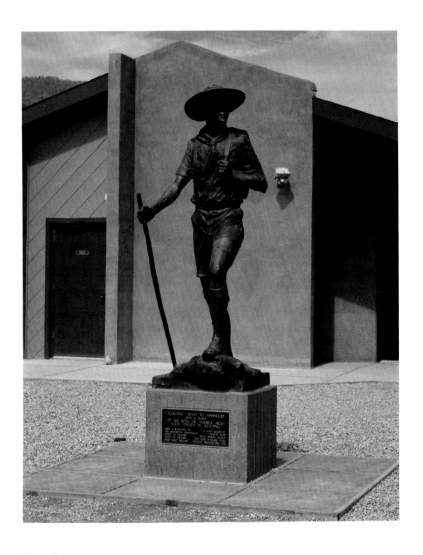

Scout bronze

Philmont awards

Clarence Dunn, who had been at Philmont in different capacities since the late 1940s, served as first Chief Ranger and directed the program until 1970. The Ranger concept was immediately successful and continues to this day. It allows crews to go directly into the backcountry and train while on the trail. Moreover, once a Ranger has prepared the crew to meet the challenges of the trail, the crew is free to develop as a cohesive unit at its own pace.

Bill Littrell, Ranch Superintendent, Ray Bryan, Manager of Phillips Properties, and Jack Rhea, Director of Camping examine a map of the ranch in the late 1950s.

Flag raising at Ponil.

A popular figure at Philmont during the 1950s was campcraft instructor R.C. "Doc" Loomis, who taught axemanship, fire building, and Dutch oven cooking. His classroom was a canvas fly and chuck box erected behind a 1935 Chevy coupe. There he held campers spellbound during a three hour presentation on the care and use of a three-quarter axe. He began with the statement, "A new axe is not ready to use," and explained by first giving each group a kit that contained a file, whetstone, sandpaper, fence staples, and linseed oil. He then showed them how to cut off the axe's fawn's foot, wedge the handle with staples, sand and linseed the handle, and finally sharpen the bit to a fine edge.

After a brief discussion about the use of a camp knife, he demonstrated fire building. He ended with detailed instruction on making biscuits in a Dutch oven. Philmont published the major portion of Doc's demonstration in a pamphlet titled, "On the Trail. . .with your Knife, Axe, and Dutch Oven," and gave a copy to all participating campers and leaders. With Doc's instruction the Scouts left Philmont with traditional outdoor skills they could use for the rest of their lives.

Doc Loomis and his demonstration of the care and use of a Philmont axe.

General Manager Jim Fitch retired in 1949 and was replaced by Deputy Chief Scout Executive Pliny Powers who directed Philmont and the Philtower until 1953. He was succeeded by Ray H. Bryan who was named assistant to the Chief Scout Executive in charge of the Phillips Properties. Bryan's previous experience with the inception of Philturn and its development gave him special insight into Philmont and Mr. Phillips' wishes for it.

Waite Phillips with Philmont campers, summer 1955.

A Philmont wrangler sings a western tune to some campers stopped along the trail.

Scouts help brand a Philmont calf in the summer of 1954.

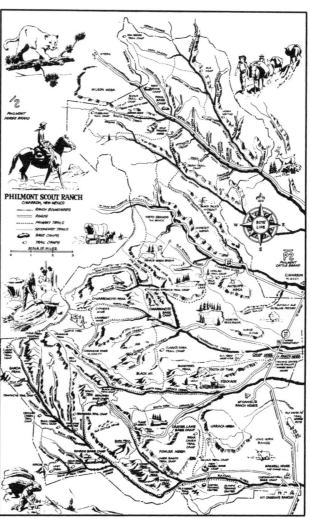

Philmont Map as it appeared in the March, 1954 issue of Boy's Life.

George Bullock left Philmont in 1954 to become Scout Executive of the Kit Carson Council, headquartered in Albuquerque. He was replaced by Jack L. Rhea who had been serving as Assistant Director of Volunteer Training at the National Office.

Attendance rose even higher in subsequent years topping 7,000 in 1954. Rhea soon found it difficult to accommodate the great number of campers in the existing schedules. Consequently, in 1956 he standardized the backcountry program into twelve-day expeditions and allowed each crew to plan its own itinerary. The new system proved to be popular because it gave crews the latitude to explore a particular area or hike the entire length of the ranch. Junior Leader and conservation training camps continued at Rayado.

One of the growing number of campers of the 1950s.

The petroglyphs in the North Ponil Canyon had been a special feature for campers since the days of Philturn. In 1956, Eugene Lutes, a former Philmont advisor and Columbia University trained archaeologist, established an excavation program at Indian Writings Camp. He led campers on tours of the petroglyphs and told them what was currently known about the prehistoric inhabitants of the canyon. He also taught them how to properly excavate an archaeological site and how to catalog the objects recovered from it. The work done by Philmont campers since that time has been invaluable in helping archaeologists reconstruct the life of the Indians that once lived in the North Ponil.

Archaeologist Gene Lutes excavates a burial at Indian Writings Camp.

1960 was a special year for Philmont and all members of the BSA since it marked the fiftieth anniversary of the movement. The Fifth National Jamboree was also held that year in Colorado Springs. More than 5,000 Jamboree Scouts and Explorers came to Philmont to hike on specially designed Jambo-treks either before or after the Jamboree.

That same year Chief Scout Executive Arthur A. Schuck renamed Clear Creek Mountain in honor of Waite Phillips, his longtime friend. In keeping with his usual modesty, Phillips had for several years been reluctant to agree to the renaming but eventually did so after much encouragement from Schuck.

Shooting .22 caliber rifles.

A Philmont mountain campsite, late 1950s.

Phillips was unable to attend the dedication held at Philmont on July 31st, a few days after the Jamboree. However, he sent a telegram to Mr. Schuck that read as follows:

"To . . . all . . . participating in the dedication ceremonies of renaming Clear Creek Mountain, I send greetings. It has been a long time since I have had the pleasure of riding my faithful old gray horse over the trails, foothills, divides, valleys, and then up the slopes of this high mountain to enjoy the majestic view from its summit. While I cannot attend in person, be assured I will be there in thought and with grateful appreciation to those who have protected and preserved this magnificent ranch for the benefit of Explorers, Scouts, and their volunteer adult leaders. Furthermore my blessings go to these Boy Scouts with the hope that they will receive as much physical betterment and mental inspiration as I did in exploring the rugged, natural beauty of Philmont. For these reasons I reaffirm my statement of 20 years ago that this property, referred to as the 'Great University of the Out-of-Doors,' should not be selfishly held for the benefit of the few but made available to the many, as nothing in the mean time has caused me to change that opinion. In conclusion, I express my cordial best wishes to you all."

A camper consults his map during a rest stop in the Miranda meadow.

As the ceremony took place at headquarters, a group of Scouts was at the summit of the mountain. There they imbedded a bronze plaque inscribed with the words, "Waite Phillips Mountain is dedicated this 31st day of July, 1960, in appreciation of Waite Phillips whose generosity has opened new horizons to the Scouts who travel the Philmont Trails."

Trail sign on the top of Mount Phillips.

In the following years Phillips suffered from poor health that culminated in a congestive heart attack in early December of 1963. He died on January 27, 1964.

Phillips' generosity to the Boy Scouts of America, however, did not end with his death. His will included a bequest of one million dollars. He directed that the money be invested and the income used to provide financial assistance to underprivileged Scouts and Explorers who wished to hike and camp at Philmont.

In 1963 Philmont was significantly enlarged with the addition of 10,098 acres of the eastern slopes of Baldy Mountain. The acreage was purchased and given to the Boy Scouts of America by Washington Scouter Norton Clapp. It was the last parcel of land yet controlled by the Maxwell Land Grant Company, and its addition gave Philmont campers access to the historic gold mining region. The Baldy country brought the ranch's total area to 137,493 acres or approximately 214 square miles.

Jack Rhea left Philmont after the 1962 camping season and was succeeded by A.J. "Skipper" Juncker, formerly director of Region VII's canoe base. Juncker's untimely death in the spring of 1965 brought Joseph J. Davis to the ranch as Director of Camping, where he remained through the 1973 season.

Philmont suffered a devastating flood in 1965. Results are still visible in many parts of the ranch. After an unusually wet spring that year, heavy rains began falling on June 14th and continued through the 18th (the planned first arrival day of campers). Rivers and creeks swelled to flood proportions. The flood waters caused extensive damage to campsites, trails, roads, and bridges especially in the south country. Rayado Canyon was the hardest hit. At Fish Camp the swollen Agua Fria Creek swept away the kitchen of the main lodge. At Rayado Camp the river was at some points more than 250 feet wide. The Junior Leader Instructor Training Staff battled high water with sandbags and saved the historic buildings at the camp.

As the waters subsided, the Philmont staff mobilized to rehabilitate the backcountry in anticipation of the arrival of campers. Rangers equipped with axes and bowsaws were sent to the backcountry to hike trails and clear or redevelop them as necessary. Other staff members rebuilt or relocated campsites. Commenting on their efforts, General Manager Bryan said, "I've never before seen such a grand 'gung-ho' attitude. This flood welded our . . . young men into the best team the ranch has ever had."

Staff members carrying supplies across Urraca Creek during the June, 1965 flood.

The number of Philmont campers rose throughout the 1960s, totaling well over 10,000 each summer in the last years of the decade. In response to those numbers a preplanned itinerary system was developed for the 1969 season. The itineraries were designated leisurely, challenging, or strenuous and provided a wide choice of programs and routes. Importantly, the system ensured that crews were evenly distributed across the ranch. The new system alleviated overcrowding in heavily used camps.

Joe Davis, Philmont's Director of Camping from 1965 to 1973, with campers at the summit of Baldy Mountain.

The itineraries were printed in booklet form and sent to Expedition leaders prior to arrival so that crews could make their choices at home and thus save time once at Camp Headquarters. In 1973 the book was named *PEAKS* or *Philmont Expedition Adventure Key to Superactivities*. The system has proved to be so popular and effective that with certain refinements it remains in use today.

During the 1960s camps were established and staffed in Philmont's backcountry to provide expedition campers with additional program opportunities. The programs ranged from geology, forestry, field biology and astronomy to burro packing, survival, and rifle and shotgun shooting. Rock climbing was offered for the first time in 1967 at Ponil Camp. The program was later offered at Cimarroncito, Dean Cow, and Miner's Park Camps.

It was during the 1960s that Philmont added a major museum facility. Ernest Thompson Seton (1860-1946) was one of the founders of the Boy Scouts of America and served as the first Chief Scout. With Lord Baden-Powell, he co-authored the first American Scout handbook. Seton was an eminent naturalist who drew and painted animals in the wild and wrote stories about their lives and behavior. He was best known for a book he wrote and illustrated, *Wild Animals I Have Known* (1898), in which he recounted the story of his capture of the notorious wolf, Lobo.

In 1965 Seton's wife, Julia, gave his library, art, and Indian artifact collection to the Boy Scouts of America. The following year L.O. Crosby, Jr., a Scouter from Picayune, Mississippi, provided funds to build a museum at Philmont in which to house the collection. It was dedicated as the Seton Memorial Library and Museum in June of 1967. Since that time other collections pertaining to the Southwest have been acquired. The Pueblo style

On the trail during the 1960s.

Ernest Thompson Seton.

building was renamed Philmont Museum and Seton Memorial Library in 1982 and offers changing exhibits that pertain to Seton's life and work and the history of the Philmont area.

In addition to High Adventure Expeditions, Philmont offers an advanced program for older Scouts. The Rayado program encompasses outdoor leadership, hiking, campcraft, and wilderness problem-solving. The program began in 1968. The first participants were called Kit Carson Men. Over 100 campers from the previous summer's regular program were selected to take part. The program proved to be a huge success. In 1973, following the first year of coed camping at Philmont, several young women participated as Kit Carson Women. The name for both programs was changed to Rayado in 1976. One of the purposes of the program was to create a reservoir of potential summer staff members. Over the years many outstanding staff members have first come to Philmont as Rayado campers.

Filling canteens at Lovers Leap spring.

In order to take part in Rayado, participants must be 15 years old by January 1 of the current year, but not yet 21. Each applicant must be recommended by the unit leader and the council and must be in excellent physical condition. Philmont's most experienced Rangers lead Rayado crews. Rayado Rangers seek to develop and enhance a participant's leadership abilities, backpacking techniques, orienteering, ecological awareness, and other camping practices. Unique individual and group experiences are also included to encourage personal growth and self-confidence. The program lasts for 15 days, with three sessions being offered each summer. The number of participants averages around one hundred.

Baking biscuits in a Dutch Oven.

A burro at Ponil Camp photographed by advisor R. Taylor Drake in 1967.

Floods that occurred in 1965 and 1969 helped bring about an important service program at Philmont. These floods severely eroded some backcountry trails and completely demolished others. It was obvious that a program devoted to trail maintenance and conservation should be developed on the ranch. The result was the establishment of the Trail Crew program in 1970. Each year approximately 60 Scouts take part in Trail Crew. Participants must be 16-years-old by January 1 of the current year but not yet 21. Crews are led by members of the summer Conservation Department staff. A participant in the program spends 14 days at a backcountry work project and then hikes on a standard High Adventure Expedition. Because there is no fee, this program gives disadvantaged Scouts the opportunity to come to Philmont. Work projects center around trail conservation and maintenance, but crews also build check

Scouts from many foreign lands have served as Philmont staff members over the years.

dams, clear away deadfall, re-seed barren areas, rebuild switchbacks and work on other conservation projects. Because trail building and maintenance is so important to the camping operation, members of regular expeditions also devote time to conservation projects while hiking at the ranch.

More programs were developed at camps in the 1970s. Among them were orienteering, bowhunting, mountain search and rescue, and Jicarilla Apache Indian ethnology. Philmont's historical legacy provided the inspiration for several interpretive programs beginning with the establishment of the Rocky Mountain Fur Trappers Company at Clear Creek Camp in 1972. There staff members dressed in costumes of the period and taught campers how mountain men trapped beaver in the fur trade days. Campers also learned to load and fire replicas of the black powder weapons used by fur trappers.

Making arrowheads at Apache Springs.

The gold mining areas near French Henry, Miranda, and Cyphers' Mine Camps provided settings where campers learned historic methods of placer and hard rock mining. Staff members in period dress also demonstrated blacksmithing and detailed the history of mining operations at each site.

At Black Mountain Camp a staff member in interpretive dress tells about pioneer life.

Campers at Beaubien, Ponil, and Clark's Fork rode horses and learned how cowboys roped and branded cattle. At Pueblano and Crater Lake Camps they climbed poles, sawed timbers, and made mine timbers and railroad ties like lumberjacks of the Philmont area had done.

Interpretive programs remain an integral part of each camper's backcountry experience. They allow participants to learn by doing. Campers, in essence, recreate history often in the very location where it occurred. They come to appreciate the

Pole climbing at Crater Lake Camp.

Packer Bob Juden and his mule string at Beaubien in 1975.

experiences of the pioneers in a way that could not be achieved in the classroom.

Although the BSA's Exploring program opened its units to coeducational participation in 1968, coed crews did not hike at Philmont until 1972. That year two female Rangers were on staff to train participating coed crews. Coeducational groups continue to hike Philmont trails and young women now make up about one-quarter of the seasonal staff.

After an absence of twenty years, Cavalcades were again offered to Philmont campers in 1978. They have since become one of Philmont's most popular programs, with reservations filled sometimes more than a year in advance. Participating Scouts spend eight days on the trail horseback and become proficient at bridling, saddling, feeding, and grooming their mounts. An important part of the program is learning how to pack camping gear on horses using a pack saddle and diamond hitch. It is an experience unequaled anywhere else in Scouting.

The 1990s saw the introduction of some new backcountry programs including: homesteading, adobe casa, mountain biking, wilderness medicine, search and rescue, astronomy and GPS technology. In addition, some itineraries moved off the ranch to hike and take part in programs in the 100,000 acre Valle Vidal area north of Philmont through a special use permit of the U.S. Forest Service.

In addition to the camping and training programs, Philmont continues today as a working cattle ranch pasturing a herd of more than 250 Hereford cows. In winter and spring the cows graze the grasslands on the east side of the ranch, where they have their calves. In May the calves are branded with Philmont's Bar PS brand. In June all cows, calves, and bulls are driven by cowboys to mountain pastures for the summer. The following September they are gathered and moved back to winter pastures where the calves, now weighing more

Two of Philmont's first coed campers pitching a tent in the Summer of 1972.

A young Scout curries his horse before going on a Cavalcade.

Under the eye of a staff member, campers take aim at Sawmill's 30.06 rifle range.

than five hundred pounds, are separated and shipped by trucks to buyers.

The ranch has more than 200 saddle horses for campers and Training Center participants to ride each summer. Horses are pastured in the canyon country of the north part of the ranch for most of the winter and are then driven to Headquarters in May for shoeing. They are separated into three strings and moved by wranglers to Beaubien, Clark's Fork, and Ponil camps for the summer.

Philmont also has more than one hundred burros that campers use to transport their gear between Ponil and Miranda camps in the summer. The Philmont buffalo herd is a popular attraction. Numbering around one hundred fifty, the buffalo are pastured west of the highway that runs from Philmont to Cimarron. Each spring some 35 to 40 of the yearling calves are processed for weekly barbecues held at the Training Center and Camping Headquarters during the summer.

To help feed the livestock, 700 acres of land near Headquarters are sewn in hay and other forage crops. The crops are irrigated with water that comes primarily from the Cimarron River and that is stored in Webster Reservoir.

Joe Hawkins came to Philmont to direct the Camping operation prior in 1974. He left after the 1976 season to become Director of Support Services at the Sam Houston Area Council. His successor was Lloyd Knutson, Scout Executive of the Evergreen Area Council in Everett, Washington.

On Ray Bryan's retirement in 1970, John L. Shutt came to the ranch as General Manager. His departure in 1973 brought about the promotion of William C. Littrell. Littrell's knowledge of the operation was unparalleled, having directed Philmont's ranch department for more than twenty years. After three years as General Manager, he was succeeded by Paul D. Claussen, who had served as Scout Executive at Tucson's Catalina Council.

During their tenure Claussen and Knutson pursued an ambitious development program at Camping Headquarters designed to better serve campers and leaders. The major projects included a services building where expeditions picked up food, tents, cooking gear, and other equipment, a News and Information Building equipped with a photography laboratory, a logistics building where trek itineraries are reviewed, a registration office, and Protestant and LDS chapels. The new facilities have helped improve service to campers in preparation for their backcountry adventure.

Claussen and Knutson both retired from the Boy Scouts of America in the spring of 1987 and C.M. "Chuck" Buenger became Philmont's General Manager. A thirty-year veteran with the Boy Scouts of America, he had been Scout Executive of the Black Hawk Area Council, Rockford, Illinois.

Buenger retired in 1993, and William Spice took the position of General Manager in April of that year. Spice began his Scouting career in 1960 and came to Philmont after serving as Scout Executive of the Clinton Valley Council in Pontiac, Michigan.

Philmont has led the BSA in teaching techniques of rock climbing and rappelling over the years.

David R. Bates, former Director of the Maine National High Adventure Base, was chosen to head Philmont's Program department. His previous experience on the ranch included nine years on the summer staff in the 1960s and another seven years as Assistant Director of Camping. Bates left Philmont in 1995 to became the Associate Director of the BSA Division in Dallas.

Frank Reigelman replaced Bates as Philmont's Director of Program. He left the ranch in 1998 to become the Director of Field Service for the National Capital Area Council in Bethesda, Maryland. On January 1, 1999, Mark Anderson was appointed to the position after serving as the Scout executive in Hot Springs, Arkansas.

After thirty-nine years of service with the Boy Scouts of America, Bill Spice retired in April of 2000. He was succeeded as Philmont's General Manager by Keith Gallaway, who had recently been serving as an Area Director for the BSA's Western Region. With new leadership at the passing of the millennium, Philmont was set to travel not only old, established trails, but blaze new ones as well.

6

Scouting Paradise

*"Every . . . Scout should have reason
for a feeling of pride
as part owner of this (ranch)."*
—Waite Phillips, 1948

Although many of Philmont's programs have changed or been added to over the years, the essential elements of a camping trip to the ranch have not. Scouts of today contend with the backcountry much as their predecessors did thirty and forty years ago. Aside from having to negotiate rough mountain terrain, the success of each group's trek is dependent on their ability to function as a team and work together. Moreover, what campers learn about themselves often proves to be as important as the skills they acquire. As such the experience not only fulfills the goals of Scouting, but meets Waite Phillips' intent in giving the ranch to the organization as well.

Today Philmont is the world's largest camping operation in terms of size and number of participants. Annually about eighteen thousand members of the BSA and their leaders hike the backcountry during a normal sixty-six day summer season. They come from every state in the nation and several foreign countries.

The twelve day High Adventure Expedition is still the major hiking and camping program at the ranch. Approximately three hundred campers and leaders arrive for the program each day. They are grouped into crews of seven to twelve members. A crew may be a chartered Scout troop, Venture crew, or provisional Council unit.

Expedition campers usually arrive before lunch and check in at the Welcome Center. After receiving an overnight tent assignment they meet their Ranger who will be with them for the next three days. The Ranger's first responsibility is to get the crew equipped and ready for the trail. Although there is much to be done, the Ranger is trained to ensure that preparations go smoothly and quickly.

At Camping Headquarters campers checkout tents, cooking gear, and other equipment and pick up their first few days of trail food. Together they sit for a photograph, and afterward each undergoes a brief medical examination conducted by Philmont's Health Lodge personnel. At some point during the day the Ranger has each crew member spread the contents of his or her pack on a ground cloth and checks everything against a standard list. The process is known as shakedown, and it ensures that each crew has the necessary equipment and clothing for the trail. Any extraneous items are then stored in lockers.

When time is available the crew leader and advisor (adult leader) review the expedition's trek itinerary with a staff member at Logistics. They also finalize arrangements for program, horse rides, food pick-ups, and bus transportation to and from the backcountry. In the evening all advisors in camp meet with Philmont staff for further orientation into what to expect while on the trail.

Lastly, the Ranger leads the crew on a tour of Headquarters including the Trading Post, the Philmont Museum and Seton Memorial Library, and the Villa Philmonte. In the evening after supper at the dining hall, crew members attend the religious services of their choice followed by a campfire presented by staff members who dramatize the historical events of Philmont's past. The first day at Philmont is long and hectic, but everyone goes to bed prepared for the adventure to come and anxious for it to begin.

After breakfast on the second day, gear is packed and the crew meets their Ranger at the Welcome Center. They are then bused to a point in the foothills where they shoulder packs and hike a short distance to the first night's camp. There the Ranger instructs the crew in the necessary hiking and camping skills required by Philmont's mountain terrain. Included are map and compass reading, trail safety, first aid, fire building, cooking, and camp sanitation.

Over the years many camping practices at Philmont have changed in response to the pressure placed on campsites by the large number of campers. Others have come about through the development of lightweight camping equipment. For example, crews of today rarely carry axes into the backcountry as their predecessors did in the 1940s and 1950s. Instead, they use bowsaws to cut wood for fires.

Moreover, the majority of cooking today is done with backpacking stoves which provide a more convenient and efficient method of cooking at high altitudes than wood fires. They are especially helpful given that there is often not enough wood available nearby in many campsites.

The emphasis of Ranger training today is on camping in a manner that causes as little disturbance to the backcountry as possible. Philmont has become a leader in teaching techniques of low impact and minimum trace camping that campers can use to benefit wherever they camp in the future.

During the training each camper and leader commits to the Philmont Wilderness Pledge which is a statement whereby each promises to do their best in preserving the backcountry through good Scout camping. In signing the Wilderness Pledge card each camper agrees, among other things, to keep Philmont litter free, conserve and use its water wisely, and properly camp in its campsites.

The next day the Ranger again hikes with the crew and helps them sharpen the skills they have learned. If assured that the crew is ready to go on its own, the Ranger returns to Headquarters the following morning to meet another expedition. The crew continues on for another nine days covering at least fifty miles. Some itineraries call for hikes of more than one hundred miles whereas most average around seventy.

Arriving back at Camping Headquarters on the twelfth day, crew members' first priority is most often a hot shower and a clean uniform. After checking the Post Office for mail from family and friends, they head for the snack bar for a well deserved ice cream and soft drinks. Next in importance is a visit to the

Trading Post to buy patches, neckerchiefs, T-shirts, and other mementos of their Philmont adventure.

Gear and equipment is packed and readied for the trip home. After supper that evening each crew attends a closing campfire where each member receives the Philmont Arrowhead Award in recognition of successful completion of the expedition. The crew in turn is presented the "WE ALL MADE IT" plaque.

The Awards campfire is the final activity where Philmont campers are together in crew organization. Invariably, each reflects on the time in the mountains and its challenges, fun, and excitement. The campfire ends with the "Philmont Hymn," and all go to their tents full of memories and a sense of accomplishment from their Scouting adventure at Philmont.

BIBLIOGRAPHY

Selected items pertaining to
Philmont Scout Ranch and the
History of the Cimarron Country

Books

Armstrong, Ruth. *The Chases of Cimarron*. Albuquerque: New Mexico Stockman, 1981.

Bogan, Samuel. *Let the Coyotes Howl*. New York: G.P. Putnam's Sons, 1946.

Brookshier, Frank. *The Burro*. Norman: University of Oklahoma Press, 1974.

—— *The Philmont Pack-Jacks*. Raton: Range Print, 1967.

Caffey, David L. *Head for the High Country*. Nashville: Abingdon Press, 1973.

Carter, Harvey L. *"Dear Old Kit"*. Norman: University of Oklahoma Press, 1968.

Cleaveland, Agnes Morley. *Satan's Paradise*. Cambridge: The Riverside Press, 1952.

Fergusson, Harvey. *Grant of Kingdom*. New York: William Morrow & Company, 1950.

Freiberger, Harriet. *Lucien Maxwell: Villiam or Visionary*. Santa Fe: Sunstone Press, 1999.

Guild, Thelma S. & Carter, Harvey L. *Kit Carson*. Lincoln: University of Nebraska Press, 1984.

Gunnerson, Dolores A. *The Jicarilla Apaches, a Study in Survival*. De Kalb: Northern Illinois Press, 1974.

Hilton, Tom. *Nevermore Cimarron, Nevermore*. Fort Worth: Western Heritage Press, 1970.

Huffman, Minor S. *High Adventure Among the Magic Mountains*. Allendale, N.J.: TIBS, INC.

Keleher, William A. *Maxwell Land Grant*. New York: Argosy-Antiquarian Ltd., 1964.

Lambert, Fred. *Bygone Days of the Old West*. Kansas City: Burton Publishing Company, 1948.

McCormick, Wilfred. *Eagle Scout*. New York: G.P. Putnam's Sons, 1952.

Murphy, Lawrence R. *Lucien Bonaparte Maxwell: Napoleon of the Southwest*. Norman: University of Oklahoma Press, 1983.

—— *Out in God's Country*. Springer: Springer Publishing Company, 1969.

—— *Philmont*. Albuquerque: University of New Mexico Press, 1972.

Pearson, Jim Berry. *The Maxwell Land Grant*. Norman: University of Oklahoma Press, 1961.

Stanley, F. *The Grant that Maxwell Bought*. Denver: World Press Publishing Company, 1952.

—— *One Half Mile from Heaven or the Cimarron Story*. Denver: World Press Publishing Company, 1949.

Sterling, Gray. *The Tooth of Time*. Francestown: Marshall Jones Company, 1955.

Stuever, Mary & Shaw, Daniel. *Philmont Fieldguide*. Santa Fe: S.S.S. & Greenbank, Inc., 1985.

Taylor, Morris F. *O.P. McMains and the Maxwell Land Grant Conflict*. Tucson: University of Arizona Press, 1979.

Tiller, Veronica E. Velarde. *The Jicarilla Apache Tribe, A History, 1846-1970*. Lincoln: University of Nebraska Press, 1983.

Wallis, Michael. *Beyond the Hills: The Journey of Waite Phillips*. Oklahoma City: Oklahoma Heritage Association, 1995.

Ward, Margaret. *Cimarron Saga*. Pampa, Texas: Pampa Print Shop, 1959.

Zimmer, Stephen, editor. *For Good or Bad: People of the Cimarron Country*. Santa Fe: Sunstone Press, 1999.

Zimmer, Stephen and Walker, Larry. *Philmont: An Illustrated History*. Irving: Boy Scouts of America, 1988.

Articles

Ackerman, R.O. "Boy Scouts and Mountain Men," *Muzzle Loader*, Vol.1, No. VI (January/February, 1975).

Adams, Ansel. "Philmont," *Boys' Life*, Vol. LII, No.10 (October, 1962).

Alderson, William. "Interpretive History Introduced in Scout Program at Philmont," *History News*, Vol.27, No.10 (October, 1972).

Alpers, Frank. "Surface Surveys of Prehistoric Ponil River Sites" *El Palacio*, Vol.70, No.4 (Winter 1963).

Anderson, Charles. "Philmont Explorer Treks," *Exploring*, Vol.3 No.5 (November,1973)

Babson, Walt. "Philmont," *Scouting*, Vol.64, No.1 (January-February, 1976).

Baker, Galen, "The Archaeology of the Park Plateau in Southeastern Colorado," *Southwestern Lore*, Vol.30, No.1 (June, 1964).

Barber, Alden. "The University of the Outdoors," *Boys' Life*, Vol. LXI, No.1 (January, 1971).

Blair, Sam. "The Philmont Experience," *Boys' Life*, Vol. LXXVII, No.2 (February, 1987).

Brown, Andrew. "Philmont Scout Ranch Helps Boys Grow Up," *National Geographic Magazine*, Vol. CX, No.3 (September, 1956).

Bullock, George. "Philmont's Calling," *Scouting*, Vol.36, No.6 (June-July, 1948).

——— "Philmont Scout Ranch," *Scouting*, Vol.39, No.2 (February, 1952).

Chapman, Hank & Toni. "Midas of New Mexico," *American West*, Vol. VIII, No. 1 (January, 1971).

Clawson, Marion. "Philmont Scout Ranch, an Intensively Managed Wilderness," *American Forests*, Vol. 74, No.5 (May, 1968).

Claussen, W. Edmunds. "Kit Carson's Hospitality Headquarters," *New Mexico Magazine*, Vol.28, No.2 (February, 1950).

Cleaveland, Norman. "Clay Allison's Cimarron," *New Mexico Magazine*, Vol.52, No.3-4 (March/April, 1974).

Collins, Patrick. "Philmont's Wild Kingdom," *Boys' Life*, Vol. LIV, No.11 (November, 1964).

Crump, Irving. "Protecting Philmont's Wildlife," *Boys' Life*, Vol. XL, No.3 (March, 1950).

Daniels, Gene. "Philmont Ranger," *Boys' Life*, Vol. LXV, No.2 (February, 1975).

Davis, Joseph J. "Try Philmont Camping - Best Brand Going," *Scouting*, Vol.58, No.1 (January/February 1970).

Doclar, Ernest. "Winter at Philmont," *Boys' Life*, Vol. LIX, No.12 (December, 1969).

Fitch, James P. "Philturn, the Camper's Paradise," *Boys' Life*, Vol. XXIX, No.6 (June, 1939).

Gale, Howard. "Pioneering Across Philmont," *Boys' Life*, Vol. XL, No.12 (December, 1950).

——— "Scouting's Home on the Range," *Boys' Life*, Vol. XL, No.10 (October, 1950).

Gibson, Tom. "Philmont After the Deluge," *Scouting*, Vol.53, No.8 (October, 1965).

Gregory, Doris. "High Adventure," *New Mexico Magazine*, Vol.37, No.7 (July, 1959).

Grossman, Herb. "Philmont Diary," *Boys' Life*, Vol. XLII, No.11 (November, 1952).

Gunnerson, James. "Apache Archaeology in Northeastern New Mexico," *American Antiquity*, Vol.34, No.1 (January, 1969).

——— "Archaeological Survey in Northeastern New Mexico," *El Palacio*, Vol.66, No.5 (October, 1959).

Haas, James. "Where the Deer and the Antelope Play," *Scouting*, Vol.52, No.4 (April, 1964).

Halter, Jon. "A British Artist Looks at Philmont," *Boys' Life*, Vol. LXII, No.11 (November, 1972).

Harrigan, Stephen. "Can the Boy Scouts Save America?" *Texas Monthly*, Vol.8, No.11 (November, 1980).

Hood, Bob. "Your Trip to Philmont," *Boys' Life*, Vol. XLVI, No.3 (March, 1956).

Huffman, Minor. "Great Philmont Scout Ranch Gives Healthful Outing to 2,282 Scouts From 9 States During Past Season," *New Mexico Stockman*, Vol.9, No.10 (October, 1944).

Hunt, Bill. ". . . they come as boys . . . and leave as men," *New Mexico Stockman*, Vol.39, No.9 (September, 1974).

Kemsley, William, Jr. "Philmont Scout Ranch," *Backpacker*, Vol.8, No.2 (April/May, 1980).

Kirkpatrick, David. "Archaeological Investigations in the Cimarron District, Northeastern New Mexico: 1929-1975," *Awanyu* Vol.4, No.3 (September, 1976).

Knutson, Lloyd. "Philmont," *Camping Magazine*, Vol.57, No.3 (January, 1985).

Larson, Parry. "Philmont's Conservation Classroom," *New Mexico Wildlife*, Vol.7, No.4 (July/August, 1964).

Looney, Ralph. "Philmont's Mountain Pioneers," *New Mexico Magazine*, Vol.44, No.6 & 7 (June/July, 1966).

Lowell, Steve. "Maxwell's Living Monument," *New Mexico Magazine*, Vol.38, No.5 (May, 1960).

Lucas, Lex, (editor). "5,000,000 Shareholders," *Scouting*, Vol.47, No.10 (December, 1959).

Lutes, Eugene. "A Marginal Prehistoric Culture of Northeastern New Mexico," *El Palacio*, Vol.66, No.2 (April, 1959).

—— "Secrets of the Canyon," *Boys' Life*, Vol. XLVII, No.6 (June, 1957).

MacPherson, Tom. "Looka Me on the Wagon Train," *Boys' Life*, Vol. XLII, No.1 (January, 1952).

McMorris, William. "Canyon People," *Boys' Life*, Vol. XLVII, No.11 (November, 1957).

—— "They Ride Herd on Philmont," *Boys' Life*, Vol. XLVII, No.12 (December, 1957).

Montgomery, C.M. "Cimarron of Wild and Woolly Fame," *New Mexico Magazine*, Vol.47, No.4 (April, 1969).

Morris, Lawton, "Philmont Ranger," *Boys' Life*, Vol. XLIX, No.6 (June, 1959)

Murphy, Lawrence. "The Beaubien and Miranda Land Grant; 1841-1846," *New Mexico Historical Review*, Vol.62, No.1 (January, 1967).

—— "Lucien B. Maxwell, the Making of a Western Legend," *Arizona and the West*, Vol.22, No.2 (Summer, 1980).

—— "Master of the Cimarron: Lucien B. Maxwell," *New Mexico Historical Review*, Vol.55, No.1 (January, 1980).

—— "Rayado: Pioneer Settlement," *New Mexico Historical Review*, Vol. XLVI, No.1 (January, 1971).

Olsen, Nancy Hall. "Philmont Horsemen," *Western Horseman*, Vol. XVII, No.4 (April, 1952).

Peterson, Robert W. "Ernest Thompson Seton - A Scouting Founder," *Scouting*, Vol.56, No.5 (May/June, 1968).

Pryce, Dick. "Miracle on Maxwell Mesa," *Scouting*, Vol.60, No.1 (January/February, 1972).

Rae, Donald. "Wrangler for a Day—Philmont Style," *Boys' Life*, Vol. LI, No.10 (October, 1961).

Roberts, Kenneth. "The Hardships of New Mexico," *Saturday Evening Post*, Vol.200 (December,1927).

Saxton, Edward. "Philmont: Scouting's High Adventure," *New Mexico Magazine*, Vol.56, No.6 (June, 1978).

Schweiker, Maxine. "We Found Scouting's Heart," *Scouting*, Vol.46, No.1 (January, 1958).

Skinner, S. Alan. "Lizard Cave: A Rock Shelter in Northeastern New Mexico," *El Palacio*, Vol.71, No.2 (Autumn, 1964).

Sloan, Bill. "An Artist Looks at Philmont," *Boys' Life*, Vol. XXIII, No.2 (February, 1983).

Stuckey, Scott. "Philmont: Scouting's Rocky Mountain Retreat," *Scouting*, Vol.72, No.1 (January/February, 1984).

Taylor, Morris F. "The Maxwell Cattle Company, 1881-1888," *New Mexico Historical Review*, Vol. XLIX, No.4 (October, 1974).

Wendorf, Fred. "The Archaeology of Northeastern New Mexico," *El Palacio*, Vol.67, No.2 (April, 1960).

West, James (editor). "Philmont Scout Ranch," *Scouting*, Vol.30, No.1 (January, 1942).

—— "35,857 Acres of Wilderness Presented for Scout Camping," *Scouting*, Vol. XXVI, No.11 (December, 1938).

Wylie, Even. "Scout Trail Westward," *Colliers*, (July 22, 1950).

Zimmer, Stephen. "Burros and Boy Scouts," *Western Horseman*, Vol. 62, No.4 (March, 1977).

—— & Walker, Larry. "A Cavalcade of Scouts," *Western Horseman*, Vol.45, No.4 (April, 1980).

—— "High Adventure Scouting," *The Western Horse*, Vol. XVII, No. V (May, 1993).

—— "Home on the Range," *New Mexico Magazine*, Vol. 74, No. 3 (April, 1996).

—— "Philmont Ranch," *Persimmon Hill*, Vol.22, No.2 (Summer, 1994).

—— "Polo Ponies of the West," *Western Horseman*, Vol.49, No.11 (November, 1984).

—— "Rod Taylor: Mountain Cowboy," *Western Horseman*, Vol. 63, No. 6 (June, 1998).

—— "Villa Philmonte: Mansion in the Wilderness," *New Mexico Architecture*, Vol. 30, No. 5 (Sept./Oct., 1989).

Miscellaneous

Annual Report of the Boy Scouts of America, 1938-1999.

McDonald, Jerry. "Sequential Land Use of the Philmont Scout Ranch Region, Northeastern New Mexico," unpublished Master's thesis, University of Texas at Austin, 1972.

Murphy, Lawrence. "Boom and Bust on Baldy Mountain, 1864-1964," unpublished Master's thesis, University of Arizona, 1964.

obituary. "Waite Phillips, 1883-1964," Scouting, Vol.52, No.4 (April, 1964).

Phillips, Waite. Correspondence, 1938-1963. Seton Memorial Library, Philmont Scout Ranch, Cimarron, New Mexico.

Phillips, Waite. "History of the Southwest and Philmont Scout Ranch," unpublished manuscript, 1948.

Philmont Scout Ranch collection, 1941-1999, Seton Memorial Library, Philmont Scout Ranch, Cimarron, New Mexico.

Philturn Rockymountain Scoutcamp collection, 1938-1941, Seton Memorial Library, Philmont Scout Ranch, Cimarron, New Mexico.

Robinson, G.D., et. al., Philmont Country: The Rocks and Landscape of a Famous New Mexico Ranch. U.S. Geological Survey Professional Paper 505, 1964.